Profile 11 – VIVIENNE ROCHE

Published as part of Gandon Editions'
PROFILES series on Irish artists (details p47).

ISBN 0946846 235

Editor          John O'Regan

Asst Editor     Nicola Dearey
Design          John O'Regan
                (© Gandon, 1999)
Production       Gandon Editions
Photography      see list of illustrations, p41
Printing         Nicholson & Bass, Belfast

Distributed by Gandon and its overseas agents

GANDON EDITIONS
Oysterhaven, Kinsale, Co Cork, Ireland

tel             +353 (0)21-770830
fax             +353 (0)21-770755
e-mail          gandon@eircom.net
web-site        www.gandon-editions.com

cover           *Wave Shadow* (detail)
                Dublin Dental Hospital, 1998-99

Publication grant-aided by
The Arts Council / An Chomhairle Ealaíon

The Arts Council
An Chomhairle Ealaíon

Profile # Vivienne Roche

GANDON EDITIONS

# Introduction

AIDAN DUNNE

VIVIENNE ROCHE HAS A WAY OF CONFOUNDING WHATEVER PRECONCEPTIONS we might bring to her work. Just when we had her down as a maker of formalist, geometric abstracts, she introduced elements of unmistakably representational imagery. When we had learned to accommodate the expanded metaphorical language this allowed her, she turned to making disconcertingly faithful studies of plants. Yet these dazzling changes of angle and idiom have occurred, by and large, within the parameters of a conventional sculptural vocabulary. That is to say, Roche is a fabricator of objects and images. She uses traditional media, albeit mildly stretching the definition to encompass functional and industrial materials such as glass, sailcloth or steel rope, as well as such mainstream fine art media as bronze. She has, incidentally, a personal preference for steel, which has a foot planted firmly in both camps.

If we were to apply to her, in terms of her own discipline, Proust's description of a writer as someone who doesn't so much create a verbal artefact as translate a text that is within them, it looks as if we are bound to run into difficulties. Surely Roche's inner text is more a succession of texts, each one exclusive of the last. In fact, charting her progress, the moment that causes most difficulty in this respect is, on the face of it, that paradigm shift in her work, which sees her move from geometric abstraction to organic representation. These terms are very broadly descriptive and tell only part of the story, but they are accurate as far as they go, and they do effectively encapsulate the issue.

Put it this way. Initially, the work seems to refer us to architectonic forms. The titles suggest wider concerns, but certainly, in terms of the works themselves, we are invited to experience sets of spatial relationships articulated by means of linear and planar arrangements of steel, glass and other closely related structural materials. And her detailed observation of architecture is underlined in series of very good watercolours. But she progressively transcends this precisely defined range of reference.

It has also become clear, though, that she doesn't simply abandon parts of her artistic vocabulary in favour of a new set of expressive possibilities. She expands and renews it. Her relationship to architecture, for example, is still intense and central. What does change, or perhaps the more accurate term is develop, is the nature of her attitude to space. Her conception of space is immeasurably more complex in 1999 than it was in 1979. From appearing to be a neutral container, it becomes something much more active. (I say 'appearing to be' because this is the way it comes across in individual works; internally, of course, she may well have already viewed it in a more involved way.) Significantly, this is evident in the way she scales and sites her sculptures.

Her work specifically addresses space as an arena, prey to the actions of various forces, with various potentialities, and within the frame of time. Space is something that contains, of course, in the sense that you place an object in a box, a sculpture in a gallery. But, for example, she continually draws our attention to gravity as a force in an enclosed environment, or to the action of atmospheric conditions in more open environments. She does so, as well, through the very constitution of the works, in the way they are delicately poised, or mobile to varying degrees, or susceptible to various forces. From being simply containing or contained, the internal, intervening and surrounding spaces become generative in themselves.

It is significant, in this regard, that her large-scale, publicly sited sculptures – which are integral to her work, rather than being interruptions to it – are exceptionally attentive to their setting. You could say that they literally locate themselves in the landscape. One effect of this way of thinking is that her pieces are very much at home in the world. This is certainly no accident. She is on record as pointing out that her move to Garrettstown heightened her awareness of the wider natural environment. And her experience of a geographical elsewhere, when she visited the Nordic countries, also heightened her sensitivity to the way particularities of place shape a culture.

It is a short step from there to suggest that her work is largely about being at home in the world, or about ways of being at home in the world. Some works, including her pieces for Dublin Castle and the Jefferson Smurfit headquarters, approach this in

terms of orientation. That is to say, reading or interpreting them entails tracing an account of their own orientation within their respective spaces and within their wider contexts in the physical world. Addressing them, we are, by implication, positioning ourselves in the world, or prompted into a realisation of being so positioned.

One way of looking at this is to say that any particular work will implicitly look beyond itself for a sense of completion, figuratively or literally. This completion may be found in the elements, in the literal role that wind, for example, plays in some sculptures. It may reside in the potential for or realisation of sound. (Some works seem to describe sound; others are capable of producing sound.) Or it may even have to do with the way a work responds over time to atmospheric conditions. Or, indeed, it might relate simply to gravity, in the way complex, suspended forms are held in delicate, vibrating balance, like living things. In some cases, as in *Tidal Erotics*, where forms beckon and couple, the idea of completion relates to emotional and sexual needs, and the satisfaction of those needs.

*Tidal Erotics* represents the most sustained and explicit example of a recurrent anthropomorphism in Roche's work, arguably indicative of why, rather than how, she took that original step to move beyond a formal language that she felt to be increasingly restrictive. It presumably reflects a desire to broach experiences previously excluded from her sculpture, or admissible only in ways she came to feel were too metaphorically remote. But an important element of *Tidal Erotics* is the recurrent emphasis on how organisms are moulded by their environment, are even structural reflections of their environment. It's not a case of either or; one entails the other. Viewed from this perspective, Roche's inner text unfolds in something like these terms: an appreciation of the abstract properties of spaces, contained and uncontained, gradually modulates to a sense of place and embodiment, a vision of life as being both within and inextricably linked to environment.

Aidan Dunne is the art critic for the *Irish Times* and has written extensively on Irish art.

*A Major*
1986, steel, 195 x 160 x 120 cm

# An Art of
# Passage

CIARÁN BENSON

THE AMERICAN PHILOSOPHER EDWARD CASEY ARGUES THAT 'A BUILDING CONDENSES A CULTURE IN one place'. Inside a building as a building there is nothing that was not intentionally put there. The traces of decision and action, calculation and compromise are everywhere. Outside, a building's presence is catalytic. A building, any building, in virgin landscape transforms the spirit of that place. Qualities previously there are edged out, others newly colonise, and one place turns into another. Human beings cannot but impose their mark on all they touch, but when they engineer and design what are to be their places, then expression becomes possible.

Throughout her career, Vivienne Roche has been an artist of place and passage. It has been a Janus-faced career, transforming the inward, transmuting the outward. This requires exacting skills. Built places cannot be positively developed by sculpture, cannot be moved on towards actualising latent possibilities, without the artist understanding the nature of buildings, their making, placing and powers, or lack of them, to effect (in the sense of 'shape') experience.

The dynamics of occupied and empty architectural spaces – inside and outside, above and below, left and right, in front and behind, largeness and smallness, roughness and smoothness – are extensions of the dynamics of the human body. Buildings are corporeal artefacts with a range of states which resonate with the wishes of those who make them and with some of those who dwell in and around them.

If ideas are scripts for action, then this particular idea ensures a productive dialogue of drawing, sculpture, architecture, perception and distinctively personal insight. All Roche's work, but notably the work of recent years, exudes a confidence that this grasp of the connections between material, space, perception and idea is now fluent and at the service of an increasingly subtle journey.

That journey begins with her travels to the sites of bridges being engineered by her father in the south of Ireland in the late 1950s and early 1960s. Much that is involved in the practicality of making stable passages across water became seeds of work that is coming to fruition in the late 1990s. That they can listen to the voices of particular flows of sea and river, that what they build conforms to the laws of physics and to the demands of economics, that the materials they choose be durable, and that what they make looks well, requires bridge-builders to be kinds of polyglot. The good ones must speak with the mathematical precision of engineers, the aesthetic sense of architects and sculptors, and at the same time be intensely respectful of how they alter the look of sea and land. That respect comes from observing and listening to water relating to the softness of earth and sand, to the hardness of rock.

Here is a key to Roche's sensibility. Her work is a metaphorical fusion of themes of time and human passage with a language of structure and texture that is deeply indebted to the precisions of engineering and architecture. This is disciplined art demanding disciplined, discerning attention. It is deeply felt, and very discrete. Its range extends with each new phase, but its elements are consistent and are all the time deepening and becoming more polished. The shape of her oeuvre is spiralling like a pearly nautilus.

Extremely attentive drawing is the armature of her thinking. Her earliest group shows included drawings, and her latest and finest show, *Tidal Erotics* in Dublin's Hugh Lane Gallery (1999), intimately combines drawing and sculpture in an extended exploration of human relationship in dialogue with the specially commissioned music of John Buckley.

Vivienne Roche's first major sculptural commission was the *Memorial to Cearbhall Ó Dálaigh* in Sneem, Co Kerry (1983). Despite its apparently minimalist abstraction, this piece in steel is actually quite figurative (like most abstract pieces). Arguing that the former president had a reason for choosing Sneem as a place in which to live, Roche identified the landscape as the source, and married what she took to be Ó Dálaigh's sense of Sneem as a place to his own place in it. Her modus operandi for this has become that for much of her subsequent work. The focus was an idea of 'a sense of landscape' and of a person for whom that sense was particularly powerful. To this she brought the idea of a wave. She took photographs of wave action on the beach at Garrettstown in Co Cork, where she lives. From these images of breaking waves she abstracted three elements for the Sneem memorial.

The first was an elongated form which referred to a specific wave action, a motion in time like human life, breaking on a bed of beach-stones. The second was higher, and referred to the wave-like mountain visible from the Sneem site, and so formed a bridge of local association. Breaking waves momentarily and distinctively form their own interiors, shell-like, and her memorial does the same. The precise core of commemoration occurs at this juncture of outside and inside, which echoes what it is to be a person. She painted the outside off-white, but each of the interior forms were separately painted with darker colours. Specific landscape and specific personhood fused, intentionally but not obviously.

The evasion of the obvious is further evident in Roche's favoured colour, grey. Grey is not for her a tonal black to white. Yellows and blues come together in grey. She feels that she does not respond to primary colours, but confines her range to darker subtler zones, within whose confinements much is happening if only one looks close and long enough. Attention is threaded on time and must be supported by patience. Despite this personal predilection for grey, her colour choices, in fact, emerge from her materials and their expressive powers. Her sail series of the 1980s (*Oasis, Layered, Blue, The Wind-Bower* and *Windflip*) were exuberantly colourful. Her bronzes and the large steel pieces may be blue, green, red, brown or grey. Her choice of grey as 'her' colour is, in fact, another homage to the sea and the sky, primal sources from which her intuitions flow.

Her work of the years subsequent to the memorial followed her ideas of time as waves of wind and sea, of life as passage and commemoration and – a new theme – of the cultural marking of time in musical experience and notation. The underlying dialectic here is always of movement and stillness, of bodies moving and stalling in space and time.

1985 saw *Airwave* installed on Penrose Quay in Cork – a large steel piece, developing the waveform in the vertical, in contrast to Sneem's more horizontal treatment. At this time, Roche also begins working small-scale, with themes that will later find more monumental realisation. In the lives of communities, bells toll for loss and warning, peal for marriage and festivity. They wave in time to social need. The meaning of bells and the visualisation of their kinetic harmonies now become a major preoccupation for Roche, opening up a rich seam which allows her explore the relationships of death and memorialisation, of wave, music and time ever more specifically and beautifully. Here also, for the first time, her work as an extension of hers, a woman's body, begins to be visible, and with it themes of sexuality. Smaller-scale works in steel like *Song Flight* (1984), *Bell No.1* (1985) and *Arc Rising* (1987) mark this emergence.

As might be expected, the influences on her work include places and people. Alexander Calder, George Rickie, Anthony Gormley, IM Pei, and the Irish-born engineer Peter Rice are all subjects of her gratitude and admiration. Time spent in Finland and Sweden in the late 1980s expanded and confirmed the range of her ideas and references. In Scandinavia, Roche found a culture in which she felt at home and one in which she immersed herself. Viking images and artefacts became a source of influence for much of her work in the late 1980s and early 1990s: the shapes for *Vendel Pair* (1989) were derived from a pair of stirrups seen in a museum; shapes of helmets or roofs fed into the shapes of bells; Nordic shrines informed pieces like *Sanctum* (1990) and *Belphegor* (1990); and the material found in early Scandinavian burial sites inspired the ideas in her 1989 show *Grave Goods*.

Her ideas grow more confident, her themes enlarge, and with them the scale of her work. Her many bells (*Bell No.1, Interval, Olde Nes, Earth Bell, Sigtuna Bell, Corkscrew Bell, Spoon Bell, Gaia, Tomb, Freyja's Bell* (Freyja being a goddess of love), *Monk Bell, Spiral Bell, Bow Bell, Helmet Bell, Avesta, Viapori Bell,* etc) from this period, in addition to being beautiful pieces, allow her to slowly develop a language for a theme that becomes central to her 1999 *Tidal Erotics* show, the dynamics of sexuality, power and transience. Here she has developed a highly personal lexicon, one that is distinctively hers yet which retains enough peripheral connectedness with a more general symbolic backdrop to be intuitively recognised. Her focus initially is on power between the sexes, and on how the balances of power might be authentically embodied in her work. The fact that in *Vendel Pair* the female form is the bigger one is not a simple-minded assertion of inverted dominance, but the outcome of an effort at balancing relationships of form.

In this lexicon of relations, the containing bell is to 'female' what the clapper is to 'male'. The bell in turn develops into the solid cone which becomes even more personally a female form, whereas the clapper metamorphoses into a hook form which is male. With these morphemes she begins to form her own increasingly personal expressions of sexual power and equality. These need to be artistically dynamic to be convincing. With moving clappers in resonating bells, the powers of movement are literal. With the work of the late 1990s, that kinetic relationship is incorporated into a more highly developed concept, realised in an original language capable of capturing all that she intends. Her recent work may use found seaweeds as their material, but 'found' here is chosen, and most nuances of Roche's work are deliberate and not accidental.

Before the range of her most recent work could be achieved, two other dimensions of her work in the 1990s needed development. One was scale, the other the means by which the viewer could approach and enter the work. During the 1990s, Roche produced in a short number of years what must be the most impressive corpus of large-scale public art works in Ireland to date. In doing so, she used the making and the installation of these large public pieces to refine how it was that she wanted individual viewers to approach and achieve the kinds of consciousness that her works try to engender.

The costs of materials and the general absence of big commissions prior to the 1990s prevented Irish artists generally from developing skills in making large public works, and, therefore, from thinking in terms of the impact of scale. Roche inventively tried to circumvent the material cost constraints by using sail-cloths to make high-impact, low-cost wind-pieces in the 1980s. Changing economic circumstances in 1990s Ireland presented her with opportunities for which she was well prepared imaginatively.

During this period, she made, amongst other works, *Liberty Bell* and *Sentinel* for St Patrick's Cathedral in Dublin, *Volte* in Limerick, *Duality of Three* in Tallaght, *Sea Garden* in Ringaskiddy, *Inclination* for the NMRC in Cork, *Plumbline* for Dublin Castle, *Triptych* for Smurfit Headquarters in Dublin, and *Wave Shadow* for the new Paul Koralek designed Dental School at Trinity College Dublin. In 1999 she also won the commission for what, after the millennium spire in Dublin, will be the largest public sculpture in Ireland, which will be sited at the southern entrance to the new Lee tunnel in Cork. This is provisionally called *Light Lines*, and resulted from a partnership with the engineering firm of Ove Arup.

Each deserves comment, since public sculptures in Ireland tend to appear on their sites without much celebration or comment, but the essay space demands selectivity. All of these pieces are expressively different and all were posed with different kinds of challenge regarding integration with existing buildings and the kinds of contribution that the sculpture itself was to make to its environment. Together they demonstrate a remarkable artistic versatility, inventiveness and integrity. Some, like Ringaskiddy and the Lee tunnel site, are wide-open windswept sites; others, like Dublin Castle, are narrow, elongated (four storeys) interior voids, and yet others, like the NMRC, are large, multi-storeyed interior voids. Some are there to be approached as pedestrians (*Belphegor*, *Sentinel*, *Duality of Three*), some to be played around and sat in (*Sea Garden*), some to be seen while waiting as a patient (*Wave Shadow*), and others to be approached in a car, while acting as a signature for a major new tunnel and possible town (*Light Lines*). Scale and point of entry are intimately linked here.

On scale, for example, *Plumbline* in Dublin Castle weighs nearly half a ton, hangs forty-four feet through four storeys of a five-storey building, and swings on a single ring. It is visible from each storey, but presents a different view, since within each angle on the form hangs its own distinct plumbline, while the entire piece is itself a plumbline. Within her own private lexicon, Roche envisages this piece, counter-cliché, as a female form filling a male space. Her thinking here is not so much in terms of body parts, but in terms of force, power, strength. The two elements of *Inclination* in the NMRC building together also weigh nearly half a ton and swing freely. One form is derived from Degas' *Miss Lala at the Cirque Fernando* (1879), and again the

relationship between both forms is one of intimacy. Both are made of sheet metal, painted or treated, whereas for *Wave Shadow*, Roche combined thick glass and patinated bronze for the elements of the piece that will cover a number of wall spaces. *Light Lines* will be a huge elliptical organic form of steel and cable with fibre-optic lighting, overhanging the river Lee.

Parallel with these huge projects, and feeding them, has been her personal, intimate project, which finds fruition in her 1999 Hugh Lane show, *Tidal Erotics*. Roche has always been an accomplished draughtswoman, but for this show she developed her drawing to virtuoso level. Because of the austerity of her usual materials – largely metal – and the obvious love of engineering and architecture in her work, it has sometimes been too hastily judged as 'cool' or 'difficult' or 'demanding'. In *Tidal*

*Erotics* no such judgement is credible. All the elements in her personal and artistic history are woven together coherently in an unusually ambitious project. Their roots can be traced to many previous works, but perhaps to none so emblematically as the 1986 work called *A-Major*, photographed on its brief beach site. Like the culture condensed in a building, Roche's many ideas are embryonically condensed in *A-Major*: the form through which the sea as permanent presence can be seen, the forked form containing the hook, the look like a fragment of musical notation, its reflective solitude in the wind, its constructive tension.

*Tidal Erotics* is a collaborative work in which Roche and the distinguished composer John Buckley created what – in addition to the individually wonderful pictorial, sculptural and musical forms constituting it – is a highly sophisticated installation, much like music must be traversed through time. The theme is the universal theme of love, longing, loss, resolution and growth. The rhythms of the tides provide the root metaphor for these universal human experiences. The seaweed forms (waxed, cast in bronze and patinated) are characters in an ancient story, newly and beautifully told. The exquisite drawings catch all the nuances of erotic relationship in the widest sense, mediated through that primeval source of it all – the sea.

In 'Omeros', Derek Walcott says beautifully in words what Roche in the language of the eye and Buckley in that of the ear say together in *Tidal Erotics*:

> I felt the foam head watching as I stroked an arm, as
> cold as its marble, then the shoulders in winter light
> in the studio attic. I said, 'Omeros',
>
> and *O* was the conch-shell's invocation, *mer* was
> both mother and sea in our Antillean patois,
> *os*, a grey bone, and the white surf as it crashes
>
> and spreads its sibilant collar on a lace shore.
> Omeros was the crunch of dry leaves, and the washes
> that echoed from a cave-mouth when the tide has ebbed.
> ...
> I saw how the surf printed its lace in patterns
> on the shore of her neck, then the lowering shallows
> of silk swirled at her ankles, like surf without noise...

As she completed *Tidal Erotics*, Roche was also engaged in completing what is one of the finest marriages of public art and architecture in recent Irish construction. Commissioned by Dublin Dental Hospital to make a large work for Paul Koralek's new building, Roche continued her exploration of waves and shoreline to produce a quite beautiful work, *Wave Shadow*, that is in harmonious conversation with the clean, bright movement of Koralek's building. The building moves back diagonally from the façade, and is centred on an atrium which is the hub of movement for both patients and staff.

Over the white walls of its four storeys, Roche has placed a work of many parts. The materials are slumped glass and bronze, the glass made by Salah Kawala. Each phase of the work comprises many elements and is read floor by floor, successively integrating into a complete, unified experience. This combination of glass and bronze turns out to be an inspired choice for expressing the quiet dynamism of waves temporarily fossilised between tides in the corruscations of sand, or conveying the protoplasmic look of planktonic forms energetically curving together through water. Some rectangular glass pieces hang more autonomously, framed by lines of bronze, and look somewhat like old bichromate-gum photographic prints, which perfectly abstract the curves of wet sand-waves and allow them to reform with changes in the incident light. The effect is cumulative as you mount the building by the stairs, each wall-piece building organically on the one below. Roche understands the mutuality of sea and shore in a profoundly observed way, and has managed through her art to bring the calming, meditative effects of that rhythmic, multi-sensory experience of being on a sandy seashore into what must be a place of anxiety for many – a dental hospital. Her characteristic insightfulness is nowhere more complete, effective and accessible than in this exquisite work.

Vivienne Roche is an artist of passage, a subtle cartographer of feeling in time and place. Her own mid-career flight is clearly upwards.

Ciarán Benson is Professor of Psychology at University College Dublin and former chairman of the Arts Council (1993-98).

*Tidal Erotics* (from *The Amen of Calm Waters*)
1999, graphite on tracing paper, 96 x 90 cm

# A Conversation with the Artist

AIDAN DUNNE

*Aidan Dunne – You live near the sea at Garrettstown. Is your studio there as well?*

Vivienne Roche – Yes. My studio is an old coach house – a building with a lot of character. This is where all the work begins and where most of it is realised, although some elements may be fabricated elsewhere.

*The drawings and sculptures that make up* Tidal Erotics *stem directly from your immediate home environment, don't they?*

Yes. From the sea. That body of work started with drawings of seaweed  washed up on the beach at Garrettstown. I had used seaweed in earlier work, almost incidentally, but with *Tidal Erotics*, it was a more conscious source. Moving water – wave patterns, and traces of water on sand – were the other elements I drew on.

*There's a strong sense of the rhythmic movement of the sea in the forms, an undulating pattern.*

Yes. Nothing is actually moving in the work, but there is a feeling of movement through water, and of the role of water in making forms. I made several open-air pieces in the early and mid-1980s about wind in the way these are about water, freestanding with cloth and steel. The wind shaped the form, billowing or falling slackly, depending on the weather. I think this interest comes from living with the weather and the sea.

*So there is an implicit movement in the* Tidal Erotics *drawings and sculptures?*

Yes. Movement is implied in the relationship between the forms. They show a gesture, a captured moment, and you know that something happened before and after that moment. The suspended and moving forms of other sculptures I have made are similar, I think, in that you see them in terms of their potential for movement. I think of all of these forms as held gestures.

*Yet sculpture can also be fluid and ethereal. I'm thinking of your most recent piece,* Wave Shadow, *in the Dublin Dental Hospital.*

The new Atrium in that building is full of light. Looking at it, I thought the structure of the glass roof created interesting patterns on the upper wall. They reminded me of the play of light on water, and that was my starting point.

*You used bronze in this piece, but in a way the most important material is glass, which you hadn't used for a long time.*

Not for about fifteen years, when I used flat glass alongside steel. That was in response to another Paul Koralek building, as it happens. Here I have used slumped glass. This kind of glass isn't cast. Instead, sheets of glass are cut and shaped to a mould. The underside picks up the texture of the mould; the upper side is smooth. The actual textures used are those made by moving water on sand, and the imagined textures of flowing water stilled.

*The presence of water is implicit in* Tidal Erotics, *and now you have the water itself in the glass of* Wave Shadow.

Yes, these works are closely related. I would also say that the forms in *Wave Shadow* look like the kind of organisms you find in the sea.

*I want to ask you about your use of seaweed in* Tidal Erotics. *Would you literally pick up pieces of seaweed as you walked along the beach?*

Yes. The seaweed was almost like a language for me, in the way I selected the forms.

*Did you tend to accumulate forms and then select?*

No. Because seaweed deteriorates quickly I had to work with it immediately. But also I knew precisely what I was looking for on the seashore. Obviously, I found things that surprised me as well. I used one big weed, about seven-by-six feet. It's a female form, and I suppose you could call that a found object. I waxed this weed very quickly, and continued to work on it over a period of seven months. It became the centrepiece in one of the four rooms of the exhibition – *The Amen of Calm Waters*.

*Are* Tidal Erotics *the most organic-looking things you've done?*

I suppose they are. But I also wanted them to be compositionally structured.

*Is that a question of combining geometric and organic qualities?*

That's true in the case of *Tidal Erotics*, which is composed in relation to the architectural space of the gallery. But in my work as a whole, there's another side to the question of combining different elements, and that's the use of materials. For example, the combination of bronze and steel... As materials, they evoke different emotional responses, which is important to me. Steel is known as a cold material, but that's not a

view I share. It's a tough, vigorous material. Bronze is seen as a warmer, softer metal. What draws me to bronze is the preparatory process of forming wax to be cast. This is in marked contrast to working steel – it's very much a primary, structural material.

*You mean that it is not cast, that a piece in steel is directly fabricated?*

Yes – cutting, welding, grinding – it's quite physical to handle.

*Wax is almost the opposite in terms of its working properties?*

It is. I build it up layer by layer, and it develops its own character. I also use it with clay, first modelling clay to the required form, then layering wax on to it – a kind of double modelling method. Making *Tidal Erotics*, I used wax directly onto the seaweed. Each piece was quite painstakingly worked, built up, pared away, and worked over in many layers. So the seaweed, including the process of its drying out and decomposing, became part of the sculpture. It provides a basis of form and an actual working material, and it's sacrificed to the final work. Burning off the wax, you burn off the seaweed. Something else about it is relevant as well, and that's its physical character, its smell, which, you know, is quite strong, especially when decomposing. So it's there all the way through, and it seems to permeate the work for me.

*Though you're based in the country, you were brought up in the city?*

Yes. In Cork. And, as a child, we went out to Garrettstown often on day trips, or to stay during the holidays. My grandparents had a summer house near the beach.

*What it is about the sea that made you want to live beside it?*

It has to do with the rhythms, the tides, the seasons. Even now, when I'm away, I look forward to going back and settling into that rhythm. It's almost like resetting my own body rhythm to it. The sea is a stabilising factor in my life.

*Isn't it true that even in Cork city, you're always near to a sense of the sea, and certainly water.*

Absolutely. In Cork, you're always aware of the complexities of the river.

*You moved to Garrettstown when the logical thing in career terms would have been to gravitate towards an urban centre.*

To some extent. But you have to remember the kind of work I do. It needs space. Living in the country was just a matter of location at first. For a decade or so after I moved to Garrettstown, my concerns remained urban. The role of architecture in shaping the urban experience, and a formalist approach to my work, generally meant that during that period my work was almost placeless. Gradually, however, the natural environment became a conscious focus. My surroundings became an imaginative as well as a literal ground. I also started to make work for specific sites, and that made me think more about a sense of place. The interaction between formalist concerns and the natural environment has been a central motor of my work in recent years. Practically and artistically, the coastal context has been crucial in shaping a personal and aesthetic perspective.

I have often thought that if I had involved myself in an urban art scene from an early age, then my professional life might have developed sooner but my aesthetic and personal maturation might have been distorted.

*You've kept up an exceptional pace of work in the 1990s.*

Yes, there have been new opportunities for making work through Percent for Art schemes and because of a more general awareness of the role of art in the built environment. In recent years, I have been able to explore a range of sculptural concerns on a large scale. I made *Sea Garden* in Ringaskiddy for Cork Harbour Commissioners, which combines fabricated sculptural forms with extensive earthworks – it's a small park, in effect. Then, in France, during l'Imaginaire Irlandais, I made a work in response to the Romanesque architecture – the bell tower, cloisters, vaulted chapel and formal gardens – of a beautiful abbey in Charroux, near Poitiers. But among the most challenging large-scale works is the series of suspended works which I made to commission over a period of three years.

*You did one such piece for Dublin Castle.*

Yes, for the Ship Street buildings in 1995. *Plumbline* is a suspended sculpture, fifteen metres long, hanging through four floors of the building. The following year I made a piece for the National Microelectronic Research Centre in UCC, which is a development of that balanced form. *Inclination* has two curving, suspended shapes, one male, one female, which are inclined towards each other and towards an implied line – the centre of the building. *Triptych*, the third and final work in this series, has three suspended forms, and is in the Smurfit headquarters in Dublin. So I went from one to two to three hanging forms, all cutting through different buildings. In every case, I was grappling with issues of perspective and balance in what I consider pure space.

*They're all very large. Do you like working on that scale?*

I do sometimes, particularly when this scale has a meaning within the overall environment of a building or its surroundings, and becomes part of the shaping of public space. Making suspended works opens up new ways of dealing with sculptural issues that are different from ground or wall-based pieces.

*How are they different?*

Well, you have all the normal sculptural concerns like line, mass, weight and shadow, but suspending a work can animate space through a more complex and subtle balance of forces than is conventionally available.

*You mean you don't work from the ground up, so to speak?*

When I work on free-standing ground pieces, my own body is the point of reference. But when I work on one of these suspended sculptures, the whole sense of scale and perspective is more complex, with multiple viewing points within a building.

This changes the feel of the work dramatically.

*In contrast to these architectural sites, you've also made large outdoor pieces, like* Sea Garden *in Ringaskiddy, for pretty much the opposite – huge open spaces exposed to the elements.*

Yes, *Sea Garden* creates a new environment rather than responding to an existing one. It's built on reclaimed land. I made it as a place to be, as an outdoor waiting room for people using the ferryport. The ground is formed into waves, hence the title.

*Do you work from direct references?*

I draw for reference, in various notebooks. Drawing can work in many ways – as a store of ideas, as a process of thinking, as an end in itself. But I also take photographs, and have done so for many years. Image and memory are well connected. I regularly photograph the beach in Garrettstown, and use these photographs in different ways, sometimes working directly from the images, sometimes as a measure of change in the environment or in my mood. I see things according to the mood I'm in.

*So, photography's a kind of combined notebook and sketchbook for you.*

Exactly, and I'll refer to the photos every so often as I would look back through a sketchbook.

*And it's a satisfactory way of working for you?*

Very. I should say that I'm not a photographer, and I don't care about the technicalities of it.

*You want to use the photographs, rather than make nice images in themselves.*

I don't set out to make a photographic image for its own sake, though at the same time, I find I often work with a composition that I've devised through a photograph. I suppose in that sense, it really is like drawing for me. *(continued on page 42)*

*Freyja's Bell*
1989, bronze, 40 x 35 x 20 cm

*Bow Bell*
1990, bronze and polished steel, 250 x 95 x 95 cm

*Steady Air*
1994, bronze and polished steel, 120 x 80 x 80 cm

*Gaia*
1992, bronze, 41 x 28 x 24 cm

*Plumb Lines II*
1994, bronze, 190 x 116 x 10 cm

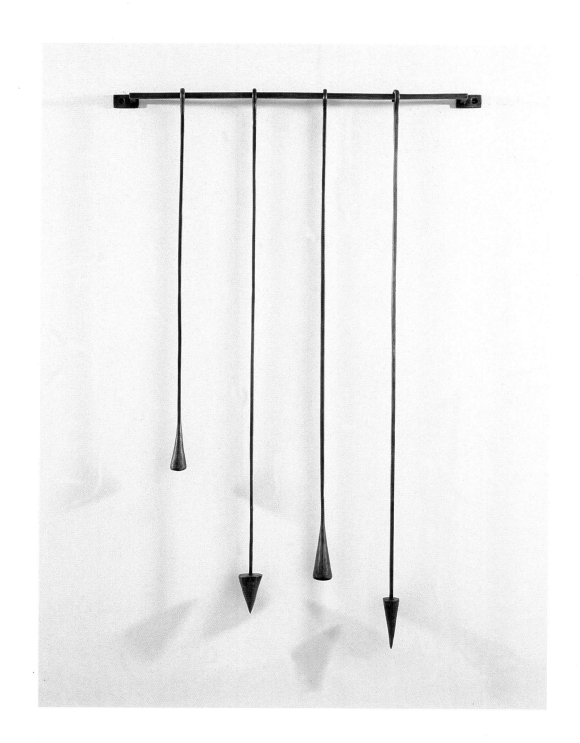

*Duality of Three*
1995, cor-ten steel, 7 x 21 x 5 m
Tallaght, Co Dublin

*Interval*
1990, polished steel and bronze
190 x 182 x 150 cm

*Liberty Bell*
1988, steel and bronze, 285 x 185 x 160 cm
St Patrick's Park, Dublin

*Sentinel*
1992-94, bronze and cast-iron, 350 x 600 x 300 cm
Patrick Street, Dublin

*Sea Garden*
1994-95, cor-ten steel, bronze, stainless steel, earthworks, 5 x 70 x 40 m
Ferry Terminal, Ringaskiddy, Co Cork

*Plumbline*
1995, painted steel, bronze, stainless steel, 14.5 x 3 x 3 m
Dublin Castle

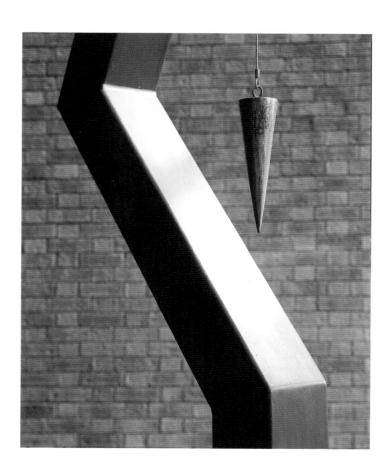

*Omphalos*

1996, installation, Charroux Abbey, near Poitiers, France

left – steel, bronze, stainless steel, 8 x 1.3 x 1.3 m

right – polished steel and bronze, 4 x 1 x 1 m

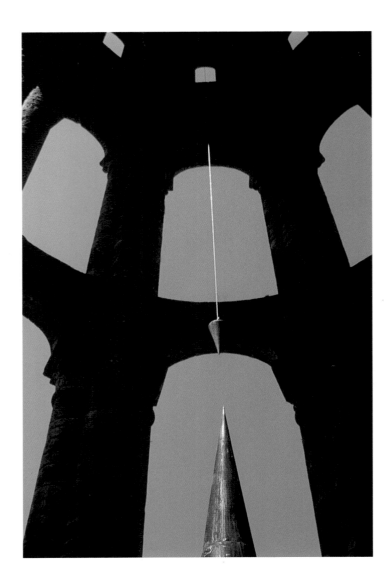

*Triptych*
1997, painted steel, bronze, brass, stainless steel, 5.2 x 3 x 2.5 m
Jefferson Smurfit Group HQ, Dublin

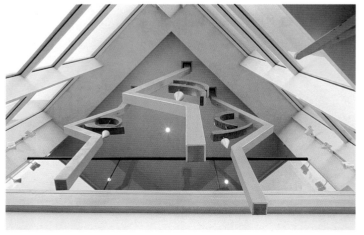

*Inclination*
1995-96, sheet bronze, cast bronze, stainless steel, 7 x 5 x 0.5 m
NMRC, University College Cork

*pages 34-35*
*Wave Shadow*
1998-99, glass and bronze
Atrium, Dublin Dental Hospital, Trinity College

 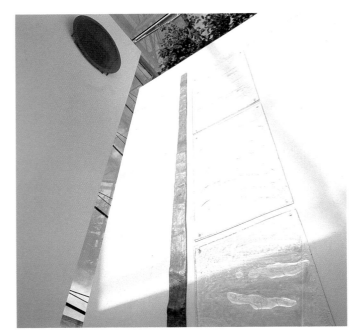

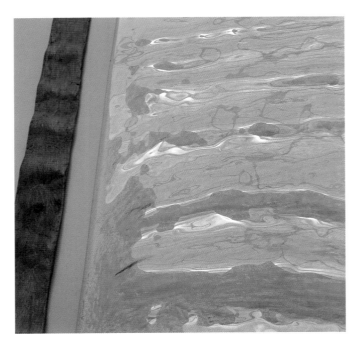 

*Tidal Erotics*
installation, Hugh Lane Municipal Gallery, Dublin, 1999

left – *Soundings*
1999, bronze, dimensions variable (detail)

right – *Coda*
1999, bronze, dimensions variable (detail)

*Tidal Erotics*
1999, bronze, dimensions variable (detail)

*Ever Drifting*
1999, bronze, dimensions variable (detail)

*Wave Shadow*
1998-99, glass and bronze (detail)
Atrium, Dublin Dental Hospital, Trinity College

photographers – JK = John Kellett / DM = Denis Mortell / VR = Vivienne Roche /
JS = John Searle (Gandon Archive) / JLT = Jean-Luc Terradillos / SV = Sakari Viika (Comet)

(continued from page 16)

*Sound has often played a significant role in your work, so there is a kind of logic to your collaboration with composer John Buckley for* Tidal Erotics.

A major early theme of my work was the forms of musical instruments, particularly those from primitive cultures. My interest in these forms led to an awareness of the sculptural possibilities of the sounds produced by bells and various kinds of percussion instruments.

With *Tidal Erotics*, music was integral to the idea of the exhibition as a time-based experience. In the Hugh Lane Gallery, the show was laid out over four rooms, and we thought of them as four movements. So there's a different sense to each room and each has its own title – *Soundings*, *Tidal Erotics*, *The Amen of Calm Waters*, and *Ever Drifting*. The rooms were composed through the three forms – sculpture, drawing and music. John and I worked together for nearly two years building up the exhibition. The collaboration worked in different ways. For instance,

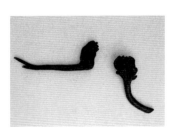

for the first room, *Soundings*, I made a series of paired forms. Then John composed a set of two-instrument pieces, and the dialogue between the instruments complements the dialogue between the paired forms on the walls.

*Why did you decide to use the paired forms rather than just working on the basis of single forms?*

That decision to use paired forms had an emotional basis actually. I wasn't interested in the shape of the material – a piece of seaweed looking like a piece of seaweed. I thought of these as male and female forms. Making connections between forms, and finding these images of sexuality, are very much the source of the work.

*Hence the title?*

Yes, it's a suggestive title. While most of the forms are either male or female, not all of the work is necessarily related to sexuality.

*In relation to the bells, they've become a regular part of your sculptural vocabulary, and their arrival was something of a landmark in your work. You've talked of them as female forms, and you could read the imagery of bell and clapper in a sexual way.*

Yes, I would say there are sexual connotations to the bells. Some bells are female for me, some clappers are male.

But I should say that those bell-forms had a variety of sources. They're related to the shapes of Viking helmets and the domed roofs of the Stockholm skyline, for example.

*Spending time in Scandinavia was pivotal for you, wasn't it?*

It was. It changed the way I thought about my work, and it changed what I began to put into the work – the whole question of work having an emotional basis. Being there allowed me to engage with that in a more direct way than I did before.

*Would you have resisted the idea previously?*

Well, I would have had mixed feelings about it. Of course, it wasn't just Scandinavia; it would be misleading to suggest that. It's more that it came at a particular time in my life; I happened to be in the right place at the right time, and it drew something out of me.

*So Scandinavia has had an enduring impact on you?*

It had a profound and direct impact on me personally and artistically when I first encountered that landscape and culture. I made a whole corpus of work based on that experience. My part of the *Edge to Edge* show, which toured Scandinavia, reflected this. I have sited work in Sweden, and many pieces which I have made in the last ten years or so have been inspired by Nordic landscape and culture.

Its lasting influence is more subtle. Strangely, I think it affects my work now most significantly in colouring my sense of light and shade. In Scandinavia I found the skies and the way the light falls on the landscape quite similar to home, but with an increased intensity. That has made me much more conscious of the play of light on the landscape and the seascape in Ireland. I felt comfortable with that distinctive light, and still revel in it here. I think because I have an affinity with the north.

*You mean north/south in terms of Mediterranean/northern Europe?*

Yes. We look more at our Celtic past, but I think our Viking roots are very strong, just understated. I certainly feel that connection personally.

*Your father was an engineer who built bridges. Obviously it's reasonable to see some link with the structural, architectonic elements in your work. As a child, were you aware of his projects?*

Yes, he designed bridges, and I would have been aware of what he was doing. Not in a very detailed way, but as a child it was part of my life, visiting sites and seeing bridges under construction. In fact, some of my earliest memories are of the two sides of bridges coming together. A lot of the bridges he worked on were concrete structures, built as replacements for steel bridges.

*Quite a convincing link, then.*

I never consciously think of it in those terms. Though I must say, I was very pleased when the possibility of doing a piece for the Lee tunnel came up. It tied in so well with what he did, and with my interest in engineering generally, that it seemed appropriate.

*That's a very ambitious plan. It will be the largest public art project in the country to date.*

*Light Lines* is a sixty-metre arc of light – fibre-optic lines on a cantilevered steel structure, counter-balanced and cable-tied to another steel form. It will embrace a bend on the river near the south entrance to the tunnel. What I'm trying to do is explore and develop the role of the river in the consciousness of the city. In the past, the river would have had a stronger recreational function than it has now, and I think it's time to look at how that role can be enhanced again. A riverside walk is being developed as part of the tunnel scheme, and at the moment I'm looking at ways the tunnel sculpture can further enhance that.

*In what sense?*

The sculpture will work in two ways: firstly, as a large-scale, very visible work marking the Jack Lynch Tunnel, and secondly, as a more personal work, one you can encounter as a pedestrian walking along the river. The challenge is to take something large and make it intimate as well. Light will play a big part here, as it changes through seasons and with events. I hope it will become a living landmark.

Aidan Dunne is the art critic for the *Irish Times* and has written extensively on Irish art.

Cáit Ward

# VIVIENNE ROCHE

| | |
|---|---|
| 1953 | Born in Cork |
| 1970-74 | Crawford School of Art, Cork |
| 1974-75 | School of the Museum of Fine Arts, Boston, USA |
| 1989 | Co-founder, National Sculpture Factory, Cork |
| 1993-98 | Member of the Arts Council / An Chomhairle Ealaíon |
| 1995 | Associate member, RHA |
| 1996 | Elected member of Aosdána |
| | Lives and works in Co Cork |

## Solo Exhibitions

| | |
|---|---|
| 2000 | *New Work*, Rubicon Gallery, Dublin |
| 1999 | *Tidal Erotics*, Hugh Lane Municipal Gallery of Modern Art, Dublin; Galway Arts Centre; Sirius Project, Cobh; Model Arts Centre, Sligo (a collaboration with composer John Buckley) |
| 1996 | *Omphalos*, installation, Charroux Abbey, near Poitiers, France (part of l'Imaginaire Irlandais) |
| 1994 | *Steady Air*, Green on Red Gallery, Dublin |
| 1992 | *Sightlines*, Crawford Municipal Art Gallery, Cork |
| 1989 | *Northern Light*, Riverrun Gallery, Dublin; Riverrun Gallery, Limerick; Garter Lane Arts Centre, Waterford *Grave Goods*, Octagon Gallery, Belfast |
| 1987 | Hendriks Gallery, Dublin (also 1980, 1983) *The Wind Bower*, installation, Bank of Ireland, Dublin |
| 1986 | AIB Bank, Cork |
| 1984 | Cork Arts Society Gallery, Cork (also 1978) |

## Selected Commissions

| | |
|---|---|
| 1999- | *Light Lines*, Lee Tunnel, Cork (in collaboration with Ove Arup) (Cork Corporation) |
| 1999 | *Wave Shadow*, Dublin Dental Hospital, Trinity College (Dublin Dental Hospital / Ahrends Burton Koralek Architects) |

| 1997 | *Triptych*, Jefferson Smurfit Group HQ, Dublin |
| 1996 | *Temple Bar Print Suite* (Temple Bar Properties) |
| 1995- | *Love Letters*, College Road, Cork (Cork Corporation) |
| 1995-96 | *Inclination*, National Microelectronic Research Centre, University College Cork |
| 1995 | *Duality of Three*, Tallaght, Co Dublin (Office of Public Works) |
| | *Plumbline*, Dublin Castle (Office of Public Works) |
| 1994-95 | *Sea Garden*, Ferry Terminal, Ringaskiddy, Co Cork (Port of Cork) |
| 1992-94 | *Sentinel*, Patrick Street, Dublin (Dublin Corporation) |
| | *Untitled*, The Green Building, Temple Bar, Dublin (Murray O'Laoire Architects) |
| 1990-91 | *Viapori Bell*, Crawford Municipal Art Gallery, Cork (Friends of the Crawford Gallery) |
| | *Volte*, Limerick Civic Centre (Limerick Corporation) |
| | *Trim Bell*, Trim Fire Station, Co Meath (Meath County Council) |
| 1989 | *Delta Curve*, Merops Ltd, Dublin |
| 1989-95 | *Lear, Volpone, Trios* (theatre sets for Meridian Theatre Company, Cork) |
| 1988 | *Liberty Bell*, St Patrick's Park (Dublin Sculpture Symposium) |
| 1985 | *Airwave*, Penrose Quay, Cork (Cork 800) |
| 1983 | National Memorial to President Cearbhall O'Dalaigh, Sneem, Co Kerry |
| 1978-79 | Coakley's Atlantic Hotel, Garrettstown, Co Cork |
| 1975-76 | Frankfield Church, Cork |

## Selected Group Exhibitions

| 1999 | *Shore*, Rubicon Gallery, Dublin |
| | *Objects in Time – artists: artefacts*, West Cork Arts Centre, Skibbereen (curated by Vivienne Roche) |
| 1998 | RHA Annual Exhibition, RHA Gallagher Gallery, Dublin (also 1992, 1996, 1997) |
| 1997 | *Small Sculptures*, Solomon Gallery, Dublin |
| | *Sense of Cork*, Cork Institute of Technology |
| | Green on Red Gallery, Dublin (also 1993, 1996) |
| 1995 | *Irish Art 1770-1995 – History and Society*, |

| | Crawford Gallery, Cork, and touring USA |
| | *Compulsive Objects*, Rubicon Gallery, Dublin |
| | Boyle Arts Festival |
| 1994 | Angela Flowers Gallery, Rosscarbery, Co Cork |
| 1991 | *Parable Island*, Bluecoat Gallery, Liverpool; Camden Arts Centre, London |
| 1990-91 | *Edge to Edge – Three Sculptors from Ireland: Eilis O'Connell, Kathy Prendergast, Vivienne Roche*, touring Finland and Sweden |
| 1988 | Hendriks/Russell Gallery, New York |
| | *EV⁺A 88*, Limerick |
| | *Heads*, Arts Council touring exhibition |

Public and Corporate Collections – AIB Bank; The Arts Council / An Chomhairle Ealaíon; Ascon Ltd, Co Kildare; BASF Ireland; Contemporary Irish Art Society; Cork Institute of Technology; Crawford Municipal Art Gallery, Cork; Guinness Peat Aviation, Limerick; Hugh Lane Municipal Gallery of Modern Art, Dublin; Insurance Corporation of Ireland; Irish Life Insurance, Dublin; Jacobs Ltd, Dublin; National Self-Portrait Collection, Limerick; Office of Public Works; University College, Cork; University College, Dublin

## Selected Bibliography

| 1999 | *Vivienne Roche – Tidal Erotics*, intro by Sebastian Barry (Hugh Lane Municipal Gallery, Dublin) |
| 1992 | *Vivienne Roche – Sightlines*, intro by Nuala Fenton (Crawford Municipal Art Gallery, Cork) |
| 1991 | *Works 2 – Vivienne Roche*, ed. John O'Regan, interview by Vera Ryan (Gandon Editions) |
| 1990 | *Edge to Edge – Three Sculptors from Ireland*, ed. John O'Regan, essay by Aidan Dunne, interview by Johnny Hanrahan (Gandon Editions) |

Vivienne Roche is represented by the Rubicon Gallery
10 St Stephen's Green, Dublin 2
(tel 01-6708055 / fax 01-6708057 / e-mail rubi@iol.ie)

Approach Road to tunnel, South

## GANDON EDITIONS

Gandon Editions is the leading producer of books on Irish art and architecture.

Gandon Editions was established in 1983 and was named after the architect James Gandon (1743-1823), as the initial focus was on architecture titles.

We now produce 20 to 25 art and architecture titles per year, both under the Gandon imprint and on behalf of a wide range of art and architectural institutions in Ireland. We have produced over 200 titles to date.

Gandon books are available from good bookshops in Ireland and abroad, or direct from:

GANDON EDITIONS
Oysterhaven, Kinsale, Co Cork, Ireland

tel          +353 (0)21-770830
fax          +353 (0)21-770755
e-mail       gandon@eircom.net
web-site     www.gandon-editions.com

## PROFILES

In 1996, Gandon Editions launched PROFILES – a series of medium-format books on contemporary Irish artists. In 1997, we launched a companion series on contemporary Irish architects. Both series are edited and designed by John O'Regan.

Each volume in the PROFILES series carries two major texts – an essay and an interview with the artist / architect – and is heavily illustrated in colour. They are of a standard design, with 48 pages in a 23 cm square format, and retail at £7.50 paperback.

To date, we have published eleven titles in the art series and three in the architecture series.

*already published*

Profile 1 – PAULINE FLYNN
essays by Paul M O'Reilly and Gus Gibney
ISBN 0946641 722   Gandon Editions, 1996

Profile 2 – SEÁN McSWEENEY
essay by Brian Fallon
interview by Aidan Dunne
ISBN 0946641 617   Gandon Editions, 1996

Profile 3 – EILÍS O'CONNELL
essay by Caoimhín Mac Giolla Léith
interview by Medb Ruane
ISBN 0946641 870   Gandon Editions, 1997

Profile 4 – SIOBÁN PIERCY
essay by Aidan Dunne
interview by Vera Ryan
ISBN 0946641 900   Gandon Editions, 1997

Profile 5 – MARY LOHAN
essay by Noel Sheridan
intro and interview by Aidan Dunne
ISBN 0946641 889   Gandon Editions, 1998

Profile 6 – ALICE MAHER
essay by Medb Ruane
interview by Medb Ruane
ISBN 0946641 935   Gandon Editions, 1998

Profile 7 – CHARLES HARPER
essay by Gerry Walker
interview by Aidan Dunne
ISBN 0946846 111   Gandon Editions, 1998

Profile 8 – MAUD COTTER
essay by Luke Clancy
interview by Luke Clancy
ISBN 0946846 073   Gandon Editions, 1998

Profile 9 – MICHEAL FARRELL
essay by Aidan Dunne
intro and interview by Gerry Walker
ISBN 0946846 138   Gandon Editions, 1998

Profile 10 – BARRIE COOKE
intro by Seamus Heaney
essay by Aidan Dunne
interview by Niall MacMonagle
ISBN 0946846 170   Gandon Editions, 1998

Profile 11 – VIVIENNE ROCHE
essay by Ciarán Benson
intro and interview by Aidan Dunne
ISBN 0946846 235   Gandon Editions, 1999

*titles in preparation*

| | |
|---|---|
| CECILY BRENNAN | BRIAN MAGUIRE |
| LOUIS LE BROCQUY | NIGEL ROLFE |
| MAURICE DESMOND | JAMES SCANLON |
| FELIM EGAN | CAMILLE SOUTER |
| ANNE MADDEN | MICHAEL WARREN |
| | *to be continued ...* |